The Anchor Holds:

Poems from the Shipwreck

by Jason Farley

Published by Jovial Press,
2106 E. 63rd, Spokane, WA 99223
www.jovial-pub.com

Printed in the United States of America

1 2 3 4 5 6 7 8 9 10   22 21 20 19 18 17

ISBN: 0-99980-505-3

ISBN-13: 978-0-9998050-5-3

FOREWORD

I used to be much more aware of my image. Always carefully curating, I only shared stories if I was the hero. It was exhausting, but I was all in on the project, so it never seemed a burden. But I have aged, and not like a fine wine. While passing through the years I have come to a conclusion. I am bad a being human.

It has been a painful conclusion to draw. When I look back, there is more that I am embarrassed of than I am proud of. I've been the clown more than the bull rider (though I have also been the bull on more occasions than I like to admit). It hasn't been pretty.

I have also found, though, that the places where I have crashed and burned, the places where my errors have left a crater, have been beacons to the people coming up behind me in ways my heroics never were. My mistakes have been beacons of hope and grace to mistake making people.

This collection of poems is organized around the parts of a ship. I did not write them with the theme in mind, but the theme was obvious to me as I read them. These last few years have been a cobbled harvest of the many fields my wife and I have been plowing through our twenty years of marriage. We were unmoored from the route we expected to sail by a disease I never expected to have before we sat in a windless sea and waited for a breeze to blow. It has been an odd time, but a good time.

Putting words to my weakness and the hopeful harnessing of God's promises has brought soul-renewal that I didn't think possible. Jesus, it turns out, is faithful and true. In storms or in silence, in work times and rest, Jesus' love is insistent that we become the person he made us to be.

I have aged. I have quit curating my image. I have become comfortable with who I am. Clowns are needed at this rodeo. I don't need to be a hero. My story already has one. I am bad at being human, but the resurrected Lion of Judah, in the Holy Ghost's windy Word-breath, still roars on my behalf.

Jason Farley
Jovial Hall, Spokane
Beaver New Moon, 2022 AD

To EEF

my Ireland
my Lizzy
my Fairest

CONTENTS

FOREWORD   I

DEDICATION   III

ANCHOR   I

SAIL   15

KEEL   33

CROW'S NEST   53

RUDDER   79

BOWSPRIT   IOI

SHIPWRECK   II3

Anchor

Home

The tender soul has fixed his love on one spot in the world;
the strong man has extended his love to all places;
the perfect man has extinguished his.
   - Hugh of St. Victor, The Didascalion

The anchor of the soul
that holds when all else is blown
by hurricanes that swirl the senses.

The smell of Halloween
— of one-pan meals —
squeezed into the betweens.

Of grief dug-deep
by three rounds with a brain tumor
and six rounds with its cure.

Of brownies given by neighbors
who would gladly give themselves
to fill the hole if they could.

Memories safe in the cilia.

Late night basement ping pong,
replacing sleep
with three-of-five
smash-and-dive brother-battles.

Home is where humanity
is made people.
Made family.
Made us.

You are not us.
But we are not less us
because of your us.

Your Gigi's perfect potatoes
do not make my Grandma's
less. Even though they're not the same.

I recognize the look
in your eyes when you remember
your dad's terrible cooking

with longing. When you laugh
about your little brother
crashing your first car, I get it.

It happened to me too.
But mine was my sister,
and it was a blown head-gasket

on my first — and only — truck.
But the feeling is the same.
The feeling that the rope still holds.

That the wind and waves
are no match
for the weight of home.

As You Wish

Have you seen it?
One of your own poets
has declared, "Life is pain, Highness.
Anyone who tells you different
is selling something." But he turned
out to be her savior in disguise.

Have you seen it?
He suffered beyond the suffering
of any man before or since
because he loved like he kissed,
more passionately than anyone
before or since, and though
they always shriek louder
when preparing to feed on human
flesh, and though Buttercup
could not fend off an R.O.U.S.,
or climb herself out of the lightning sand,
the Dread Pirate Farm Boy
has been developing an immunity
to iocane powder.
Also, he is not left-handed.

Have you seen it?
Buttercup cannot overpower the pig

Humperdinck and his perfect ears.
So miracle Max and his wife
— who is not even sure
she wants to be that anymore —
coats the resurrection in chocolate
so that — though it is inconceivable —
it will go down easier.

Have you seen it?
The four white horsemen
of the apocalypse
of the mostly dead
break free of the pit of despair
to have fun storming the castle
where they are offered gold
and power, all that is had and more,
but all they want
is their father back
"You son of a bitch,"
and a princess
pure and lovely,
since may-wage
may-wage is what
bwings us togeffa
today.

So I ask you,
have you seen it?
Have you seen it?
Anybody want a peanut?

Raspberry Pie

Bent over raspberry pie,
my tongue the taproot of my soul.
Gems jammed and canned,
sounding themselves in the crushing.
Rushing to the world, sweetening
the pie. Glorifying snowmelt
and sunshine. Tiny sun-run harvesters,
wide loads running row on row
of wind. Sweetening the Spirit-breath
so it can samba down my tastebuds.
Stomp the Paso Doble up the edges,
the red cape of the bull-fighter
folded into the butter-flaked crust.
Alabaster flask of raspberry juice,
fork-cracked to anoint the mouth's alleys,
flow up the root system,
and feed my soul.

Tested by Battle

Their leader unlocked the lid of his word-hoard
And spoke words of silver, summoning wisdom.
- Beowulf, Fifth Fitt, Lines 260-261

Strong-minded, high-hearted,
tested by battle.
Steel-knit soul-bones
with strength of deep mountains.
Anchored by crosses
in a strong hand-harbor,
wisdom's not well-known,
but nevertheless silver.

A broadly-heaped word-hoard
dug deep by the speaker.
Kept against dragon's teeth
and the tongue of the reaper.
High-hearted — beholden —
held firm by the knowing.
Gem-crusted, golden
deep waters keep flowing.
Our leader unlocked
the lid of his word-hoard.
Wisdom, steel-knit,
as our soul's bed and board.

Love Holds

There is a rhythm and a rhyme to our story
the glory of a living and a felt allegory.

> Sometimes the rain comes down
> to fill all the wells while we drown.

And now we know that even full loaded our love holds,
it won't fold when the storms of life blow.

> Sometimes the rain comes down
> and overflows the banks of our town.

And when our trials deep-draw us into this seed grave,
we have already been saved from a lead wave.

> Sometimes the rain comes down
> to water all the lives underground.

There is a rhythm and a rhyme to our story.
The quarry of love's survived stormy glory.

> Sometimes the rain comes down
> to fill the wells while we drown.

A Thing of Beauty

A thing of beauty is a joy in the moment.
Its loveliness drills down, though it passes
into nothingness. Though music's moment
glorifies the time. The quiet returns and sound
will sleep. And dreams, mysterious, even with
our breath, settle with the silent hours of sleep.
Therefore, each new morning brings breathings
of new mercies. A crown horned with passing
moments, which lift us from the earth.
As beauty aeries our eyes, ennobles away
our inhumanity through both bright
and gloom-filled passing days.
Moments made for pointing, moments
open to the breeze of eternity's freshening
wind. Some shape of beauty moves, hips
ledged to balance new life, which, for
a moment, will lift the pall. Such the
moon, dancing on the waters, swinging
like tree-tires. Old, sturdy, more
than half way gone. Old shade for bright
spirits and simple passing sheep.

Haiku #1

Hospitality,
sourdough from God to man.
Wine has to ferment.

Tomato Plants

My thirsty tomato plants
dig into the soil, grasping at the firmness
of the well-packed soil. Dry soil
is firm, but deadly. When the sun rises
the leaves whisper, the fruit
gets hard. It gets bitter.
Its flowers become small green stones.
But in the soil, soft with rain
the grip is unsure, but the fruit
becomes globes of sweet
ready to be sliced for summer burgers
or diced for fellowship's salsa.
The firmer the grasp the roots hold in the soil
the firmer the grasp the soil has on the roots.

Sail

Ode to the East Wind

O easy East wind, the breath of lengthening days.
You, from whom unseen the spirit of Easter springs
green, like sprites of life, from an enchanted sleep
waking, bright, and pink, a trumpet gold sleep.
Prophecy-woken multitudes: O you,
the charioteer of the wine-dark morning spears
of light and life, You swallow cold and warm the soil,
watch seed like a corpse within its grave, until
the fingers, green and grasping, grip the surface
and ring the morning in o'er dreaming earth.
The waking bees, that hum and whistle at their work
consummate the love of flower and tree, filling
all the air with smells of wood and dirt.
Wild Spirit, you are moving everywhere
resurrecting and renewing; Hear. O hear.

Breathing Windows

Weave, weave the sunlight in your hair.
-T.S. Eliot

The stained-glass window bends
and colors the light,
playing with what
it can't produce.

There were three in the meadow
by the brook. Letting the warmth
through. Windows
with fishing poles.
Catching and cleaning trout.
Filling them with honey.
Resting fish
on burned down coals.
Tipped lamps.
Jars of clay,
with high-pressured hairline cracks
made means of shine.

Light escaping the fowler's net
through the windows,
to be bent
and colored.
Light to warm in,

hot cocoa in hand,
as marshmallows bob on top,
until, eventually they melt
into the milk-chocolate to be sipped.
Slowly and thoroughly enjoyed.

The Scars of God's Hands

For Justin Spencer

My soul clung to the dust,
now dust clings to my soul.
Your life-breath, once blown
up the nose of my father,
once exhaled in fruit-statutes,
once blown across the dry bones
until they got up
to dance; breathe life
on me. Speak again the six
stanzas that climb up to rest.
Speak them into me. Tie
my ears to my dusty soul
and blow.

I, clay-jar, am
cracked. Scratched. Divoted. Grand
Canyons that leak. But, Lord, if
my scars leak out,
might they leak in?
If I am not air tight,
might your breath
sneak in?

Can scars be glory?
Can glory leave scars?
I will run to my heart's end.
Enlarge my heart.
Might your scarred love
love the scarred?
Let your scarred hands
leave scars.
Blow. Blow hard enough
to dislodge the dust.
Even if it takes a hurricane.
Even if it leaves scars.

Stay in the Dance-Fight

Fire in the heavens
all flowing down,
dissolving.
Testing the metal
to see what can pass
through the heat.
The shoulders of Jesus
with feet like brass
are the safest place
for his little brothers and sisters.

Jesus, dancing on the hot coals
of the burning heavens
and the melting elements,
knows how to lead
the New Heavens and the New Earth
into roundy reels.
The steeple bells still ring in the wells.
Lady Justice will line up for the electric slide.
Sophie will Tango with Logos.
Credenda will swing Agenda in their square.
And Jesus, bobbing to the beat
spins the record
that keeps the block bumping

until the conga line
is formed, with Christ
at the head, setting the rhythm,
guiding the steps.
Forging the path we follow
through the dance floor,
setting the theatre of God's glory
aflame with his moves.

And he is not ashamed
to have us in his crew.
He laughs with us as we learn the steps.
He smiles when we step on his heels.
It is not our dance
that make justice flow down
like streams of living water.
We only "therefore" dance.

He danced down the sun, moon, and stars,
sparks flying from his heels.
The elements melted with the fervent heat.
We just conga across the coals
with the Lord of the Dance in the lead.

John the Baptizer

Camel-haired and Locust-breathed.
Wild-eyed honey-tongued prophet
preaching home-towns to wild-lands.
Deserts into orchard rows.

Eyes like fire, through beard, like wire,
"Repent and flee from Egypt's
garden, gather past the water
'fore the locusts pick it clean.

Preaching like a sword is swung,
like shovel tip stabs desert soil,
or camel feet tread down the scrub,
his honeyed tongue whipped out sharp grace.

And desert-hearts drank baptism's rain
and locust-lives purge up their sin
under the eyes of the prophet's gaze.
Only the exiled find the wilderness a cousin.

Solitude

Never lonely, never alone.
Always surrounded by the celebrating
crowds, smiling and joyous,
pressing in, pressing on.

Never alone, never lonely.
Beautiful people's breath
misting the air, heating the cold
room, drinks, like fire, lick the tongue.

Thumping songs, karate-
kicking my brain into submission.
Surrounded by hot-breathed ladies and gentlemen,
never alone, always lonely.

The social treadmill, ramping up
drawing down, doubling down
with flames licking up our heels.
Always alone. Always lonely.

Welcome Home

When the father sees his son
he runs to him...
runs to him.
The scorn-filled village eyes shifting
from son to father,
past waiting for civilities.

Hands stretched wide
enough to hug the world
of this young man.
This broken young man.
This broken young slave.
His broken young son.

Arms spread in spectacle. A cross
the yard like this? When else has such mercy walked?
In the cool of the morning
— past the fig trees and fruit vines —
no heart to wait for the right time
or for church bells to chime.
Let the whole world whisper.
Divine love is divine.

Howl

Like evening wolves
that leave nothing for the morning,
the judges of the land
eat up the poor
and the orphans
— The unprotected —
from the shards of ice
thrown into their gardens
and the tubes slid down
the gas tanks of their tractors
to steal fuel.

But, lowly on a donkey,
the rightful king!
A priest after
the order of Melkizedek.
A prophet after
the order of Elijah.
A son, like Solomon,
of their father David.
A patriarch after
the order of Joseph,
unrecognized,
throw down a well-grave
by his brothers. Rejected

to the right-hand
of the Ruler of all, (Hosanna!)
the King of kings, (Hosanna!)
the Lord of lords, Hosanna!
Blessed is he who comes
in the name of the Lord.
It cannot be that a prophet can die
away from Jerusalem.

Woe to the oppressing and rebellious city
whose prophets are fickle
and feckless men
who do violence
to the law.
Your legs
are too clumsy to kickbox
with God, and too short
to race him.

Curvy Love

Like a mountain meadow echo returning,
    you turn and fill my eyes with a yearning.
Like the slender ankled daughters of ocean
    your banks and curves they give you your motion.

Streams bubble down the falls like a bard, then
    flowing through the trees and into the garden.
The way you see the world and its notions
    gives me a clearly marked out path to devotion.

Flee, Pursue, Fight, Keep
1 Tim. 6:11-16

To flee is to pursue.
There is no other way.
To pursue a steadfast love
is to grasp a gentle faith.

To fight the fight of faith
takes a fierce and firm meek soul.
Take a grip on life eternal
and remain unstained and whole.

To keep the Lord's commandments
is to want life over death.
The law describes the life of God,
the throne of thrones, the light of light,
the resurrected Lord of Life.
Come live on by His breath.

Invisible

The waters deep within the earth
—dark-delved in rounded wells—
plunk and splash because they are
themselves. Seen or unseen they are
themselves. The fullness deep-dwells
in the unshining shadows, sleek
like sneaking panthers, tree creepers
slinking in the hanging vines,
on mossed branches, unseen.
They are themselves.
Existence does not lean on my eyes.
The singing reeds don't need my ears,
but only the winds to whisper
a whistle to dissolve in choiring.

Haiku #2

The Baker's thumbs press
the extra air from the dough.
Preacher, preach Jesus!

Like Lembas

Like Lembas, the billboards of God's grace
grow in rows on both sides of the road.
It waves in the wind, flipping sweet
into the air. Into the atmosphere.
Fruits and grains that strengthen and sustain
my faith. The sun sines and the rain falls
on the just and unjust. Kindness
congeals into reds and greens,
is fresh-squeezed into sins and aged
into dancing. It only takes
a little to get me through a day,
and yet each day is overflowing
with Lembas.

Keel

Grace Never Wobbles

Experience is not uniform,
yet the power of Jesus compels
that the small Christ-soaked moments,
the Mercuries and moons,
and the double-weighted times,
the Saturns and the Jupiters,
each still grip and orbit the Sun.

Or else our life's purchase
will be a field of blood. Exchange
our silvers for a place to burst our bowels.
An earth released from orbit,
rather than a planet freed to wander,
will only darken and die.

The Christ-haunted sunlight,
sneaking into the sky, hides
in regularity and dependability.
The ghost of resurrection in plain sight.
Experience is not uniform,
but the grace of Jesus never wobbles.

Fixer Upper

Psalm 77 - For Corey McEachran

We are all fixer-uppers
unaware of the depth
of the projects scope.

We never plan aright.
Money pits deeper
than our pockets.

The foundation, cracked
and crumbling,
is also tilted.

The walls, dirty and peeling,
mold and rot
while hiding melting wires.

Leaking rusting pipes
creep under floors,
growling, spitting, hunting.

But leaning wall each
invite the Contractor's
touch.

Even demolition day
requires hands stretched
and hammers swung.

The plumber who piped
the Red Sea aside, who poured
firm paths in the deep,

He left his footprints
in the concrete.
Because he was there.

The Language of Honeybees

What if honeybees can talk
but they know the limits of speech.
They understand that some pleasures
are beyond words. They spend all day
flitting from flower to flower
tasting beauty, licking shades of glory
and they have discovered
where word bump against their lids
and become useless to wrangle certain joys.
So they dance
the truth to one another.

What if they can speak
but what they need to say
is beyond phonemes. What if
it can only be said
in the bumping and bouncing
beats of their bee bodies,
dancing the directions
to the depths of beauty.
Some portents
can only be wiggled and shimmied.
Some signs can only be lifted by mambo.

What if tasting the shades
of splendor in a field of flowers
would make anybody dance?

On Starting a New Screenplay
Psalm 31

The chain of shame has distressed my soul.
The shame in their eyes is like pointed swords.

For your name I am your servant.
For your name you lead and guide me,

to where I am surrounded. To life, spent
with sorrow. Through these years of sighing.

I am a broken vessel. Forgotten and destroyed.
Forgotten, though not by you? Right?

For the rite declares anew, you
Lord, my rock and refuge.

Be my rock. Be rock and refuge.
Let the lying lips be mute. Let the whispering

tongue, be pierced. The scheming-skull, let it be crushed.
Lord let me show your abundant goodness

before the children of Adam. But hide
and cover, stone and shelter me,

from the strife of tongues. Hide me
from Adam's — and Adam-within-me's — plots.

Let me be in the plot of the second Adam.
Let me leap in his land and his plan.

The chain of shame has distressed my soul;
raised the value with wisdom's gold.

You have filled my heart with rejoicing.
Give my mouth a story to speak.

Fountain and Cistern
Jer. 2:13

The fountain of fresh, clean freezing water
powerfully pumps from depths of earth's pillars
The deep wells can draw for the thirsty to drink
But the aquifer, though full, is unseen without faith.

Our surface level cisterns, are visible, but shallow.
They crack under the pressure and heat of life's plight.
When the earth's weight quakes and wobbles on its pillars
but the fountain still flows while the cisterns all drain.

Haiku #3

The leaking bucket
does not need a stronger tap.
Greet one another.

Sound Doctrine

Sound Doctrine is…wholesome, that which actually feeds souls.
- John Calvin, commenting on Titus 2

Meat and potatoes,
slow smoked and long baked.
Spiced and sliced,
plated and placed,
is good for the soul.
It has substance.
It's not dessert
first because vegetables,
salted and roasted
with garlic and peppers
are sweeter than candy.
Sliced pineapples,
baked pears
home-soured bread,
hot enough to melt
my sweet cream butter.

You know I love you.
Feed my sheep.

Swimming Lessons

*The suspicions of failed hope in the past
cast a shadow over every promise in the present,
but faith in God's promises rests on God's Character.*
-Rev. Matt Allhands

"Jump, Honey. I'll catch you."
Toes, white with gripping fear
edged across the pool's side
inch up to trust's tipping point.

That point when going back
is worse that going in.
Coaxed forward with the promise,
"Jump, Honey. I'll catch you."

A command containing an identity
and an assuring oath.
You are sweetness. My sweetness.
The bees buzzed from beauty to beauty

tasting the glory that can only be danced.
I'll catch yo my golden sugar. You can trust
me. My arms are stretch.
They are for you. To you. They are yours.

I command you, jump. Test the truth,
that you are Honey. These the promise
that my arms are towards you.
Jump, Honey. I'll catch you.

Known in the Breaking of Bread

They had even seen a vision of angels,
who said that he was alive. Luke 24:23b

The globe was once wrapped in thistles and thorns
the womb was wrapped in pain
the serpent's seed was enthroned on the air
and once the world was death-curse held.

The dragon once came, slinking, spitting
poisonous lies from his murder-held heart
and tongue, he once roamed
the world with Adam's crown.

But the dragon slaying, curse-swallowing
gardener-King came to be
wrapped in thorns
wrapped in pain
listen into the air
wrapped in death
wrapped in grave-clothes
to rap on a tomb
whose rolled-stone door
was sealed with the authority
of the king of the world.

While God sat in the heavens
and laughed. And his laughter
shook the foundations of the deep.
And his laughter shook
the thrones of the earth
and his laughter rolled back
the rock and shook the drown
from the dragon's head.

So that the Son of God, after
folding the facecloth and setting
it aside, could pick up the crown
shine it up, and add it to the crown of thorns
sitting on his smiling brow
known in the breaking of bread.

Gathered With These Saints

To gather with these selving saints
— that man, who drinks too much,
that young nervous woman,
that one who makes others nervous —
are dissolved together in 4/4 time.

The harmony of these, my pew-people, reflects
the future, invisible to the eyes,
that can be smelled
in the dance of the stars,

heard in the heavenly music
of these saints, standing for the Assurance
of Pardon and Hymn of Response.

That Rock was Christ

God, the rock, struck
by the Moses-swung rod.
The law-giving, curse-sharpening
rule of the water-splitter.
The strike of the stone
cracked the curse of the drought.
As the wandering grumblers
drunk the waters of life
from the rock that they followed

God, the Shepherd, lead his people
through the waters of birthing,
the cloud of Shekinah, the sea
of new-naming

To the Eucharistic meal
of manna and rock-water.
Feeding on Christ
at the crossroads of judgment.

Times of refreshing

There is a spring that shoots six feet,
straight and horizontal
from a granite cliff above an ice-melt lake
that is one-fifth of Five Lakes Butte.
A quarter size hole flows to feed
a perfect reflection of heaven's
deep blues and white clouds.
Clear is an understatement.
Cold doesn't communicate the tase.
Decades since the roof of my mouth
still remembers the moment the dust
that camouflaged by constancy
was cleansed by the clear and the cold.
The mud was washed away by clean water
for the first time.
When the taste buds have always been clogged
you don't know what you don't know.
Until fresh water flows over the tongue
and rinses away the generations of dirt
that have established empires at the entrances
of our throats. But once the times of refreshing
have come, the layer of sawdust suddenly gains a taste.

Invisible by omnipresence,
exhaustion is everywhere. Relief is rare
but there is a spring, clear, cold, and clean
that flows from the side of a rock,
a perfect reflection of the heavens.

Crow's Nest

Caroling

I want to believe. To see
the unseen; the unseeable.
To pierce through to the apocalypse.

To shout ollie, ollie, oxen free
to that which was hidden
from the foundation of the world.

To point through the horizon
and just beyond it, left of the sun,
right and up from the moon.

"Do you see it? New creation?
It's right there, balanced on three
legs, and one. The mirror uncracked?

Do you see
what I see?"
I want to sherpa

the masses into their future
in advance. I want to believe.
To see.

Midlife Career Change

Midway through the journey of life,
stuck between careers,
—needy for provision—

the world gobbles and roars.
"Feed me on green and greed.
Turn back from desire and settle."

The devil tempts me to despair
as work and bills peel apart.
"If my work doesn't pay, then Who?"

But that circus tiger desire
growls and purrs and the piles of words
burning in hoops as Jesus calls, "Leap!"

Christ, the wilder of the tame,
cracking his whip, giving wine,
making dangerous the lame,

calling us up beyond our eyes.
Past the lies the horizon tells,
up where Icarus could never fly

on wings made from hands
that formed and fed idols.
To us, to me, He says, "Fly."

I have often intended to come to you...

When we settle with God at the edge of our imagination,
we miss out on what God has for us, since he has laid out
for his people the whole weight of glory,
which is far beyond what we can imagine.
-Rev. Matt Allhands

The fields are gold and green
on both sides of the highway
as the hops press and pop
on their wires, hoping for harvest.

Aspiring to a boiling baptism;
to be mashed and melded with barley,
then beered by the yeasts blown in
on the wind and tracked in on shod feet.

First taste is ripe barleywine, straight
from the mash, bottled, aged until capped
bubbles impatiently waiting to gather a head
of beership between moment-bound men.

Distilled by flame, precisely applied, into
fire-water, aged with an oak-herder's patience.
Jews and gentiles, Greeks and barbarians
disagree on everything but whiskey.

With the water of life they agree,
the glory is worth the weight.

Strife?

To crooked eyes truth may wear a rye face. - Gandalf

The presence of Christ creates strife.
Death cannot have fellowship with life.
The knife of the surgeon, to the tumor, feels
like an enemy. Rife with hate, love reels.
Seals death with dancing joy.
A bitter old man hates the life of a boy.

The shadows hiss and strike at light
and such conflict is a blessing, not a slight.
A kite flown in the thunder and lightning
will be frightening to the kite. But rain might bring
dry things new life. Field dust needs water
for seed grip to take root and feed God's daughter.

The mere presence, though it's never mere,
insist that no one remain here. All must and will
follow or flee. There is no in-between for the seer.
For, false or true, with Him, we are prophets still.

Quiet Paws
2 Pet. 3:8-10
Divine forbearance is never divine inaction
or divine indifference.
-Rev. J Kyle Parker

The Lion that stalks its prey
in the long grass, like a thief
waiting for the house to empty
and the lights to go out,
slinks in the shade.
His patience, his slow moving paws,
his quiet steps, his sleep fur
like dry grass, might look like indifference
to the uninitiated. Until he brings down
the sun, moon, and stars
with a roar. The stalking lion
moves slow, as some count slowness,
but his prey knows otherwise.

On the Other Side

Let him be Easter
in us, we this city.
Where the rooster's throat crowed thrice.
Where the Ides of March
echo and return.
Where star-crossed brothers
lay in wait for one-another.

Yet, he is
still Easter
for us, though
these days are lent
as they lengthen and thicken,
brighten and broaden
as citizens keep entering.

The hundred and fifty-three
are on the other side
of crucifixion. Ten and seven
triangulated, revealing restoration.
Fished from darkness, netted
piled and sorted, gutted into pairs
and paired with loaves,
to be miracled out,
broken and passed around

to feed four or five
thousand. His reign rolls,
my rare-dear city.
So let him be Easter.

Pretend it's a city

By faith we know
that the waterfall of life
tumbles down the Sunday pulpit
flows down the aisles
through the pews;
where Auntie plays peek-a-boo
with the baby in front of her;
where a teenager wonders
if anyone will notice
his shiny new kicks;
through the dad hoping
no one noticed
his frustration at the bounces
in his horde's hearts;
and out the church doors, framed
by the steeple of solid word
a cross-tipped arrow pointing
to heaven; and down
the streets of the city
floating angels,
who paddle with their wings
to keep from bumping
the trees of life

growing in the flowing
whose leaves heal
cities, who's fruit
finally satiates our hungry.

Balaam's Donkey

Sin is always feigning to do something else.
- J Kyle Parker

The donkey has been sorely used.
The only thing in the public mind
is that he is stubborn.
When your neighbor is being an ass,
it is only the negative stereotype
of the lonely ass that is meant.
It is never the noble ass.
It is never the principled ass.
Stubbornness in the face of evil
is called courage. Stubbornness
in the face of overwhelming odds
is called nobility. We forget
the donkey that saved Balaam.
The ass that sat, refusing to move
under the wizards violent hand.
He saved the man with his stubbornness;
spoke truth under a hanging sword.
He blessed the one who was cursing him.
Lonely in his nobility the ass sat back
on his principles and refused to move.
Or the foal that walked its Lord
down the road and up the path
to the throne of God and of David.

A steed more noble than any warhorse,
Humble. A sign of the peace of victory
and the fierceness of true domesticity.
The victorious carpenter riding
to build a house for His name
behind the beautiful large ears
that sit like laurels
on the wise head
of the noble ass.

Helen Keller

When asked if she wanted sight more than anything in the world, Keller responded, "No! No! I would rather walk with a friend in the dark than walk alone in the light."

I walk all alone in the Darkness
separated from my neighbors who see.
But I walk in constant night with God
there's no better place to be.

I walk all alone in my deafness
shut off from neighbors who hear.
But in the depths of silence I speak with God.
This silence I share.

To have all my sight and be able to hear
To walk with my neighbors and talk with them there,
but not have the company and speech of my God
would be loneliness I could not bear.

Man's Chief End

Man's chief end is praise and pleasure
like the moon's dual-poled orbit
We are held to our humanity
by liturgy and joy. As the stars and planets
dance through their service, powered
by pleasure, loving their lives
of calendrical churching. Declaring,
proclaiming, the pleasure of praise.

At God's right hand
our Cantor sits smiling,
conducting us home
to praise, and
to pleasure.

Haiku #4

Hope's dark horizon
settles to cover life's eyes.
"Guess who?" sings the voice.

For Abby on Her 16th

Nōn est ad astra molli ē terris via.
There is no easy way from earth to the stars.
-Seneca Minor

My dear, you will reach the stars,
and take your place among them.
I have no doubt that a light you'll be
and each star will be a rung.
I will see when you have clung and strung them.

But even a ladder that reaches the sky
has two points touching the earth.
And climbing to the loftiest pinnacle
begins with the worth of the dirt.
First the ground must ground us down with mirth.

I've watched you work with all you have;
embracing the task at hand.
But watching you climb up a ladder of lumens
that creaks and sinks in sand,
is better than simply staying here on the land.

Heavenly Magicians

Eastern astrologers
reading star-charted Truth.
Oestra's true North.
Best-laid fourth-day
planetary-plans
on display.

The sky-inspired epiphany,
the travel plans that followed
— Isaiah 'twas foretold it,
not by looking, but by listening, up —
it was Easter in advance.
Gentiles raised to Oestrians.
Deaf ears star-drilled.
The powerful, humbled
up to their knees, and back
into their humanity.

The Mid-Winter-Spring of history
gifted gold, incense, and myrrh,
was learning to walk
in a Bethlehem house.

Flexing new fingers.
Forging fine-motor skills.
Preparing to palm
the Seven Wandering stars.

Haiku #5

Hopeless darkness fills
the night and covers the path.
Stars form constellations.

Suckling the Life of the Logos

Humanity, suckling the life of the Logos.
Wandering planets, lost in our left hand.
Self-exiled by sin, self-blinded by darkness
and oedipal eyes. We embraced ignorance.

But light loved the lepers
— covering eyes instead of sons —
light pierced the shadows and dark was overcome.
Expatriate of darkness'
kingdom, citizened by our conquerer.

There is no conflict-free
kingdom. Not while conflicted hearts,
conflicted minds, conflicted lusts are gathered.
But the light sheds light-yoked hope.

Fly-Fishing for Salmon

For Rev. J. Kyle Parker

Pink fleshed stream-seraphim
swimming upstream.
Resisting the flow
of the bobbing dead
who only fall;
who never fly.

Pushing up to leave
seed where it will be safe.
Pressing to lay roe
that'll invade the barbarous
seas, peopled by fin and shell.
from swirling harbors.

Juggernaut Fury

Their juggernaut fury bore then, breakneck, on.
—Iliad, bk 16, ln 702

A horde of chub, toddling out of time.
Marching in and out of unbalanced lines.
Terror of little lives just recently begun.
Anyone with a sense of time
sees in these wobbling ankles a rising sun.

All Chronos' alms, gathered in grinding arms
are melted into pounding pegs. Fallow farms,
alarmed by infancy, are waiting to be plowed
by multiplying energy. New Adams, healing harms,
seeing bunks peopled and barns cowed.

For the future is owned by those who keep
their children on the mission. They will reap
a harvest who have planted more than seed.
The deed on future leaders isn't steep.
Just love the ones that you must also feed.

Haiku #6

The prophets all spoke
of promised seeds, sons, and kings.
The rich don't bounce checks.

By Faith they Saw

In spite of history, we ignore God's grace
and don't believe.
-Rev. J. Kyle Parker

The twelve went out to see
a land well fortified
a land well promised
a land of milk and honey.

The ten saw giants and forgot
the ten plagues that brought down pharaoh
the ten saw the walls of Jericho
and returned to report their forgetfulness.

The two remembered gravity.
That God had chained the angels
that God had promised Abraham
and the fall of the giants echoed in the ears

in advance. They began decorating
the houses they didn't build.
They returned to report their memory,
and what they could see by it.

Rudder

The Heart is Funny

There is nothing left to do but be grateful.
— Rev. J. Kyle Parker

The heart is funny,
full or empty,
deceitful, powerful.
An engine and a steering wheel both.
My wants, my will,
my selving rhetorician.
My I. My me. My him.

An empty heart,
—a meaning vacuum—
sucks in the whole
world around us,
Leaving the shell, hollow
echoing in meaninglessness.
But full hearts find and fill.

Stuff is stuffed. Walls become windows,
stains stained-glass, as eyes are opened
by love that desires the Source of the spring.

The Faith of Cheese

Milk plus patience
matures to cheese.
Swiss, cheddar, gruyere
are the wisdoms hidden
in milk's promised future.
Knowing which wisdom
is fitting — whether the need at hand
is a shredded hard Italian
or a spreadable Dutch —
is a matter of experience.
The wisdom makes itself known
in the pallet's harmonies.
in the familiar comfort
or astonishment and surprise
of well-paired milk
with a history
and it's proper moment.

Suffering (Someday) Understood

For Bill Stutzman

Suffering, seen rightly,
is suffering seen through.
Time's telescope to
the hope of glory
hidden in the future's new.
Suffering, enfolded in,
clears the fog of time.
Winds of suffering
spirit away the mists
and melt the rime.
Faith breathes in present pain
to blow the haze away
and see the seed's gossiping
of spring-green hope in the clay.

Suffering amplifies
Death's clicking, creeping steps.
A window opened
for glory's breeze
to blow resurrection's breath
from coming time
into now's depths.
The first fruits of relief,
— of all things then made new —

can only be cut
with the sickle of suffering,
can only be harvested as an amber clue.

Feeding frequently on these firstfruits
makes us soft, welcoming, chubby.
Full and ready to feed.
To fill our tables with comfort-fruit
and make the champagne bubbly.

A Virgin Shall Be With Child

God was not reacting to circumstances.
The birth of Jesus was providential.
Rev. Voddie Bauchum

Time was full.
Full to bursting.
Full to overflowing.
The fullness of the Godhead
dwelt in him bodily.
So that time, so full
Could be filled and be full.

Adam sunk his fangs
into time's Adam's apple
Draining it, empty.
But God, who is rich in mercy,
did not let time
rot in his grave.

He blew new life
into Cronos' corpse
with a wind-promise of seed.
Planted in time
that grew, until time
was full
to bursting

So Mary, full to bursting
walked past a full inn
to fill a manger
with seraphim song
and shepherd's praise.
A full seed, planted in secret
to fill the world in time.

Titus 2:11

All of history is enticed
between two mountains,
into a valley,
doubly encliffed.

Forced forward like dance steps,
allured along the rhythms
of the bass line and boom-chuck
of the Spirit's drums.

There Grace,
hides in ambush.
Prepped to strike
with salvation.

Poised to topple
every slave-selling idol.
Ready to reveal
every scapegoating lie.

We, as worldlings, had no chance.
God the ambush-expert
drew us right
where he wanted us.

In the Flicker

We live in the flicker. - Joseph Conrad

We live in the flicker
'tween bright and deep shadow

Between all the salt
of the seas and the stream.

Fresh. Like swift burbling water
we're built for great beauty.

Nobility's bottle is full
of the smoke and years

of tears.

Ordinary Love

There is nothing ordinary
about our ordinary love
Most common fact of history
and a mystery unheard of.

For twenty years I've loved the view.
Your lips, your hips, your eyes,
your thighs. I love you.
Being yours, it satisfies.
I'm still surprised.

Dancing in the kitchen,
every year a little older,
my venus with a dishtowel
draped damp over your left shoulder.

Same hips that rocked my babies
are my handles, swinging, keeping time.
Heating oven, hinting maybe,
to a rhythm and a rhyme.
True parsley, sage, rosemary, and thyme.

When you let me put a ring on your finger,
a kid making promises without knowing
I loved my own feelings that lingered,
but my love still needed sowing.
It was seed in need of plowing,
planting. Dead love only tethered by vowing.
Grew again as a vine that would flower
in the eventide of life, love piles higher.
Twenty years and I know you more.
Twenty years and I love you more.
Twenty years and I want you more
now than I ever have before

Watching you pull garden weeds
in our backyard and in our kids
and then fill the soil with gracious seed
it is a straight full solar eclipse.

When we boarded this train I was young,
too young to know what I'd won,
to know how blessed I'd become,
that I could die like Simeon
and watch you outstrip the sun.

When you let me put a ring on your finger,
a kid making promises without knowing
I loved my own feelings that would linger
But my love it still needed sowing.
It was only seed needing plowing,
planting. Dead love only tethered by vowing.
Grew again as a vine that would flower.
In the eventide of life, love piles higher.
Twenty years and I know you more.
Twenty years and I love you more.
Twenty years and I want you more
now than I ever have before.

Peace and Quiet
1 Tim. 2:1-3

Peace and quiet.
Surprising goals.
Not adventure? Not intensity?
But God-like? Dignified?

It is the God that made the sun
—hot enough to melt and burn—
perfectly consistent.
Always right on time.
The God who stretched the giraffe
and gave the monkey
a prehensile tail,
also tilted the poles right-perfect.
He placed the moon
for surfable tides.

Perhaps prayers for quiet,
prayers for a peaceable life,
for a god-like and dignified life,
are prayers that the rhythms

of creative work and rest
remain uninterrupted;
that we might seek the welfare
— be the welfare — of the cities
of God and of man.

Priest Lake

I
Lifted from the Lake
the mid-winter fog
freezes to gleams of glitter
floating in fleeting winks.
The warmth of the water
creates a middle with the winter.
Autumn's late heat is held
long into freeze, like Christmas
apple pie served straight
from the oven, our eyes
can taste the sunlight
bent through the frozen
fog-drops floating.

II
Each spring the lake kneels
so the streams can lay hands
and lift it into robes
of green and gold. Spring
sun rises to reflect
a collar across the neck
of Mosquito Bay. Rainbow
trout peak to feast
on newborn nymphs. The first flies

of the new season. Splashing bumps
rippling the reflection between
me and the new morning
and her mercies.

III
Acres of teenage skin
warmed by summer sun
on display for each other's eye
as the first garden echoes
off the beach's sand.

New adults gather like peahens
and cocks, to smile and flirt
and crush and boast
and Adam-and-Eve at one another.
And the lake lifts his hands
to bless the visions
that trace the curves
of the shores and back roads.

Dominus Vobiscum;
Et cum spiritu tuo
eirene pasi.

Members, offered through water
immersed in chicken fights

and raised in knots, tied
through the sun-fired forge
where sand becomes
a glass through which
now-forming families
are seen darkly
and blessed truly.

IV
Early morning mirror glass
is cut into angle-wakes of waves.
The wind that whispers
through the treetops
blows into the nose of a new day.
The residue of a thousand BBQs
tickles the memory though the cilia.
Winter hides under Zephyr's skirt
Knowing *Auld Tumnus* will turn to her
with longing eyes and move
close enough to create a middle
to reach across.

Simeon's Song

For my eyes have seen your salvation. Luke 2:30

What I could not see when it was still
coming, nor while it was still
happening, I came to see when I was still.
The blindness, it turns out, was the whirl
within me, my own soul-swirl.

You've let your servant depart in peace.
My pieces puzzled together
by these deft fingers. Stretching
from where I hold Him swaddled
to pull my beard,

the world-light brightening his eyes, twinkling
the swaddled glory of his people, He sees. A revelation
to swaddle the gentiles.
What I could not see
when the silent night was still,

as I stood to serve and wait, I see
in scrunch, and scooch, smile
and stillness. I have seen the dead
raised, exiles end, babies born,
and born again. Now I hold these bills,

fight for hope, and pray. My eyes have seen
your salvation. May I see it still.
Could I have had more?
Perhaps,
I'll never know.

Smoke Filled Jars

Psalm 56:8

Smoke filled jars
line the walls of my story.
So many burned bridges, charred houses,
moments scorched to the ground.

The smoke is saved
because the one who knows
cares. He lets nothing but the sin be forgotten.
He stores the smoke eucatastrophically.

Haiku #7

"It's the Lord," he said
before swimming towards Jesus.
Grace cooks on charcoal.

Bowsprit

Suggestions for Carl Sandburg

Do you make suggestions to Carl Sandburg?
Or just let him be?
If you see something in a poem, do you peer edit?
Or, as it were, non-peer edit?
Does the poet's canonical authority
extend to the verbal inspiration,
all of the way down to the letters?

Or do *The Greats* make mistakes?
Does greatness' ledger have that column?
Perhaps greatness is not an absence
of error, but instead a presence.
A temporary lack of distance.
Word-bridges, built
so we can feel
together, see
together. Lonely
together. A presence of being.

Do you make suggestions to Carl Sandburg?
Or let him be?

Angels in the Trees

Angels perch, hidden in the shadows
of the leaves, almost visible in the branches.
As the leaves wave like flags
in the wind, whipping across the field,

they wait for their orders
to ride in in wrath through the streets
of the wicked, their swords sharpened
by a love of justice

and the whetstone of righteousness.
Never mistake God's patience
for apathy with avarice.
His judges flex their knuckles

gripping and ungripping their weapons
waiting for their orders
as the leaves wave like flags
in the wind, whipping across the field.

The Snake and the Hog

Apathy and distraction,
like a snake and a biting hog,
divide our selves into fractions,

into smaller and deeper bogs.
We sink into the python's throat
losing the continent in acres of fog.

Apathy's saliva comes to coat
and numb our abilities and our senses
and we become a droning note.

The biting pig breaks down fences
as long as we leave it with life.
When we get it onto the slaughtering bench

it will squirm and squeal while under the knife
or play dead like leaf-litter frog
but distraction fills our soul with strife,

and must be brutally unwound from the cogs.
slaughtered for bacon
tossed out like Gog and Magog.

Jungle-Judged Ziggurats

When I see jungle ruins
covered in vines like vipers
I wonder: What gods did they try
to appease? Did they sacrifice virgins?
Did it come to that?
And did those virgins
go stoically, resigned to their fate,
or were they dragged dramatically
chained and screaming?

When their high place
was melted like wax
and their idols proved powerless
to hold back the chaos
of the creeping jungle,
when the carvings
of their hands
were crumbled by the jungle's
stretching snake-fingers,
did they wonder if they should
have served a different god,
backed a different horse?
Or did they figured that everything
—even gods—have their limits,
reach the end of their powers,

get chewed up by Chronos
and conquered by Chaos,
get jungle-buried back to brutality.

Or did they get philosophical?
Did they ponder the metaphysics?
Is there an unmoved mover?
A creator, hungry for nothing
who waters the wilds,
feeds the feathered,
whispers resurrection
to the seed in his soil-grave.
Who can heal the whole
-hearted hunger
with his love
and lack of
have too?

A God who needs no virgins.
Who fills from his fullness.

I wonder if they wondered,
or if they just became cynics
who surmised it was simply
in the nature of divinity
to break promises,
to fail their followers.

Dead-Life

The self-indulgent is dead even while she lives (1 Tim. 5:6).

Zombie life is no life at all.
Leprous souls spotted
with death hunks, shedding
skin and smells. Chunks

of rot left like bread crumbs
wherever you've been.
Brain-slurping self-indulgence,
dead-life, grave-lived. Slaves

of desire.

Floundering in a Pile

Legalism and licentiousness:
monozygotic
root-twins from birth.
Rejecting the giftness of life.

The givenness
of stuff.
Hunting God's death
to avoid
sending thank you cards.

What begins together also ends together.
Especially in a three-legged race.
The antinomian pharisee
breaks the red ribbon
of disgrace and deep shame.

Postmodern actualization
of our deceitful heart's hopes.
Living deep the lies.
Tying flies for the next
expedition.

Estranged job training, drawing
others in for the illusion
of corporate justification.
Floundering in a pile
is still floundering
alone.

On Trying to Read
Shakespeare in the Dark
in the Campsite Outhouse

I have heard that Shakespeare is universal,
that he connects the particulars
of Elizabethan England
with the universals
of what it means to be human.
Of course, I've also seen the evidence.
The best Julius Caesar
is set in South Africa.
The rich skin of Mark Antony
glimmers to declare the ambition of Caesar
and moves the masses' heart and mind.
I smelled the smoke as Macbeth burned down
his family food truck
over inheritance and glory.
Some times are dark.
If you can't see
what Shakespeare is pointing at
and pointing out, it is probably
not the play. The times are dark.
Or you are blind.
I am in the dark.
I should light a match.

Snort

…and you snort at it (Mal. 1:13).

The words that are spoken
can be sculpted and formed.
A smile can be worn
under pretenses broken.
The eyes can be wise
to the heart's ill-intent.
But the nose?
The nose cannot lie.

In snorto veritas.
A snort is the truth.

Shipwreck

And He Charged Them, Saying, "Take Heed, Beware the Leaven of the Pharisees, and the Leaven of Herod"

Wait.

Who
brought
lunch?

Bring Your Shipwreck

*"The Church is like a great ship sailing the sea of the world and
tossed by the waves of temptation in this life."*
St. Boniface, letter 78

From the heart's first beat,
you need received grace.
Grace that you have never given.
Grace that you can't yet return.
You were born needy;
born unable to take care of yourself.

Born a fountain
of sin and beauty.
Sin and beauty, intermixed,
interwoven. Inseparable
to all but the scalpel
that is body-spirit sharp.
Sin and beauty simply waiting
for you — to grow —
to mark your world.
Waiting for your strength
to build or tear down.

Then God gives us all
to broken people.
To needy people.

He gives us to crooked,
to kinked, to bent people
to raise us and train us,
to teach and to nurture us.
And we — in our helplessness
and sin,
our vulnerability
and beauty —
are a gift to them.
And they are a gift to us.

We each receive grace
that we have never given
before we can ever return it.
We are fed, warmed, loved,
and taught to sail our lives
on the seas of life.
Each of us
is taught to sail by the captain
of a shipwreck.
And we each proceed
to to run aground.

Inexperienced sailors,
trained by failed sailors
and, without exception,
we shipwreck our life.

We call from our shipwrecks
to our children and friends,
"There are rocks here;
rocks there. I know."
In humility, we hope
our confession will shine.
A lighthouse to the later.
We hope that they sail further.

But each of us is a failed sailor,
floating on our shipwreck's leftovers.
We paddle our beam
our mast, our wheel, together
to worship.
But the God of Storms
works.
He picks up our shipwrecks,
mounts our mangles together,
and builds a new boat.
One brings boards for the hull,
another a mast,
another a rudder.
The Filler of Seas lashes them together
with frayed, briny rope.
The Wind-Wrangler sews together
our tatters of torn canvas

into piled patchwork,
stained with blood,
stained and tears,
stained with years of salted grief,
to catch the winds
of the breath of God,
and sail.

Each shipwreck leaves the right pieces,
remove the right pieces
and fit us into God's shipyard.
We are all broken people.
On our honest days we know it.
But God is building a church,
all made out of shipwrecks.
Because our God loves,
our God builds us into one another.
Lashing us together
like foremast and flying jib.

You might have broken yours,
but someone else has oars.
Together we'll make a whole ship.
It may seem at times
like the knot will not hold.
By sight we are always
taking on too much water.

Sharks circle the ship
but God is our navigator.
Church your crashed
and shattered life.
Others need your broken parts
to be made whole.